A ROOKIE BIOGRAPHY

# THOMAS JEFFERSON

## *Author, Inventor, President*

By Carol Greene

CHILDRENS PRESS ®
CHICAGO

*This book is for Betsy Bankhead Mackey and Jeannine Bankhead Hall Osborn.*

**Thomas Jefferson (1743-1826)**

**Library of Congress Cataloging-in-Publication Data**

Greene, Carol.
    Thomas Jefferson : author, inventor, president / by Carol Greene.
      p.   cm. — (A Rookie biography)
    Includes index.
    Summary: Describes the life of the third American president, who was
an accomplished statesman, author, and inventor.
    ISBN 0-516-04224-6
    1. Jefferson, Thomas, 1743-1826—Juvenile literature. 2. Presidents—
United States—Biography—Juvenile literature. [1. Jefferson, Thomas,
1743-1826. 2. Presidents.] I. Title. II. Series: Greene, Carol. Rookie
biography.
E332.79.G74   1991
973.4'6'092—dc20
[B]                                91-16363
                                            CIP
                                            AC

Thomas Jefferson
was a real person.
He lived from 1743 to 1826.
Jefferson did many things
to help the young
United States of America
and was its third president.
This is his story.

## TABLE OF CONTENTS

218618

The Jefferson family farm was named Shadwell. This house now stands on the Jefferson land near Charlottesville, Virginia.

# Chapter 1

# Young Tom Jefferson

Young Tom Jefferson crept
quietly through the forest.
All at once, he stopped
and knelt down.

There, on a leaf, sat a bug—
a different kind of bug—
one Tom had never seen before.

Tom watched the bug
for a long time and
wrote down what he saw.
It wasn't schoolwork.
He just wanted to learn
all he could about that bug.

Learning was important
to young Tom Jefferson.

At school, Tom learned
to read, to write,
and to do arithmetic.
But in the forests
near his Virginia home,
he learned about nature.

A mill on the Jefferson family farm

Tom ran home to tell
someone about the bug.
His father was busy
working on their farm.
His mother was busy
with her young children.

But his big sister,
Jane, listened to him.
She always had time for Tom.

7

When Tom was 9,
he went away to school.
When he was 14,
his father died.
Life was harder then,
but Tom still went to school.

Of course, he had fun too.
Sometimes he and his friend,
Dabney, acted silly.

Dabney had a fast horse.
Tom had a slow one.
But Tom made a bet
that his horse could
beat Dabney's horse
in a race on February 30.

Tom won that bet.
(There is no February 30.)

When Tom was just 16,
he went away to the
College of William and Mary
in Williamsburg, Virginia.

The College of William and Mary as it looked in Jefferson's time

At that time, America was
made up of colonies
that belonged to England.
Williamsburg was the capital
of the colony of Virginia.

Williamsburg, Virginia, has been rebuilt. Today it looks
the way it did when Thomas Jefferson lived there.

The Governor's Mansion in Williamsburg, Virginia

Tom met the governor
who ruled Virginia for England.
Tom played the violin.
He and the governor
and two other men
made music together.

But Tom studied too
—15 hours every day.
Learning was still important
to young Tom Jefferson.

Thomas Jefferson became a lawyer in 1767.

# Chapter 2

# Beginnings

After two years of college,
Tom decided that he
wanted to be a lawyer.
So he worked for five years
in a friend's law office.

Then he passed his exam
and became a lawyer.
He was a good one.
But Tom wanted to learn
about other things, too.

He read about how to
plan and build buildings.
Then he began to build
his own house near the farm
where he grew up.

The house sat on
a little mountain,
so Tom called it Monticello.
*Monticello* means
"little mountain" in Italian.

Then Tom was elected to
the House of Burgesses.
They spoke for the people
of the colony of Virginia.
Once again, Tom spent
time in Williamsburg.

Thomas Jefferson drew the plans for the main house at Monticello.

He met a girl, Martha.
She was smart and pretty,
and she loved music.

Tom and Martha got
married on January 1, 1772,
and he took her to Monticello.
It had only one room then.
But Martha knew that Tom
would finish it someday.

Right now, his mind was
busy with other things.
More and more people
thought England was unfair
to the American colonies.
They wanted to be free.

The Revolutionary War
began in 1775.
People from each colony
met to talk about
becoming a new country.
Tom came for Virginia.

# TO ALL BRAVE, HEALTHY, ABLE BODIED, AND WELL DISPOSED YOUNG MEN,

IN THIS NEIGHBOURHOOD, WHO HAVE ANY INCLINATION TO JOIN THE TROOPS,
NOW RAISING UNDER

## GENERAL WASHINGTON,

FOR THE DEFENCE OF THE

### LIBERTIES AND INDEPENDENCE

OF THE UNITED STATES,

Against the hostile designs of foreign enemies,

# TAKE NOTICE,

THAT

Tuesday, Wednesday, Thursday, Friday and Saturday at Spotswood in
Middlesex county, attendance will be given by
Lieutenant _____ Recruiting _____ with his music and recruiting party of _____ company in _____ Wayn Shute
Battalion of the 11th regiment of infantry, commanded by Lieutenant Colonel Aaron Ogden, for the purpose of receiving the enrollment of such youth of SPIRIT, as may be willing to enter into this HONOURABLE service.

The ENCOURAGEMENT at this time, to enlist, is truly liberal and generous, namely, a bounty of TWELVE dollars, an annual and fully sufficient supply of good and handsome cloathing, a daily allowance of a large and ample ration of provisions, together with SIXTY dollars a year in GOLD and SILVER money on account of pay, the whole of which the soldier may lay up for himself and friends, as all articles proper for his subsistance and comfort are provided by law, without any expence to him.

Those who may favour this recruiting party with their attendance as above, will have an opportunity of hearing and seeing in a more particular manner, the great advantages which these brave men will have, who shall embrace this opportunity of spending a few happy years in viewing the different parts of this beautiful continent, in the honourable and truly respectable character of a soldier, after which, he may, if he pleases return home to his friends, with his pockets FULL of money and his head COVER'D with laurels.

GOD SAVE THE UNITED STATES.

A public notice (left) calling for colonists to join Washington's army. The Battle of Lexington (below) was the first battle of the Revolutionary War.

The group asked Tom
to write something that
would tell the world
they were free now.
Tom wrote the
Declaration of Independence.

Jefferson worked long hours writing
the Declaration of Independence.
You can see how many changes he
made to the Declaration (below)
before he was happy with what he wrote.

The signing of the Declaration of Independence

On July 4, 1776,
the people who had met
adopted the Declaration.
That was the
first Independence Day
of the United States of America.

When Thomas Jefferson was governor of Virginia, the lawmakers met in the old state capitol (below).

# Chapter 3

# Problems

A new country has
many problems to solve.
Thomas Jefferson helped
the United States do that.

First, he worked for
better laws in Virginia.
He helped pass a law
that gave people the right
to choose their own religion.
He was proud of that law.

From 1779 to 1781, Jefferson
was governor of Virginia.

Later he wrote a book,
*Notes on the State of Virginia.*
In it, he wrote about
geography, plants, and animals.

He wrote about other things, too.
He said slavery was wrong.
He said the Indians
had been treated unfairly.
He said most wars were foolish.

In 1782, a terrible thing
happened to Jefferson's family.
His wife, Martha, died.

Jefferson was sick with grief.
He stayed in his room
for three long weeks.
Then he roamed the forests
and rode his horse.
Nothing helped his pain.

But he had two
little girls,
Martha and Mary.
They needed
their father.
So Jefferson
made himself
get better
for their sake.

Martha
Jefferson (left)
was called
Patsy by
her father.
Her sister
Mary was
called Polly.

In 1783, he was elected to
the Continental Congress.
There he figured out
the system of money
that we still use today.

In 1785, President Washington
asked Jefferson to be
minister to France.
He took Martha with him
and Mary came later.

In France, Jefferson helped
other countries understand
that the United States
was a fine new country.

He told them about the land,
the plants, and the animals.
He got them to trade goods
with the United States.

Jefferson also found plants
to take home with him.
He liked to try new things.

Thomas Jefferson
was one of the
first farmers
to grow tomatoes
in the United States.

George Washington's first Cabinet: (left to right) Henry Knox,
Thomas Jefferson, Alexander Hamilton, and Edmund Randolph

In 1789, he came home.
He became George Washington's
first secretary of state.
That was a big job
with big problems.

The secretary of the treasury,
Alexander Hamilton, said
rich people should run
the U.S. government.
Jefferson said the government
belonged to all the people.

Other people took sides.
Soon there were two parties.
Jefferson ran for president
against John Adams,
one of Hamilton's people.

Jefferson lost,  but he
became vice president.
That was how elections
worked in those days.
Jefferson went on
fighting for his ideas.

Thomas Jefferson became the third president
of the United States in 1801.

# Chapter 4

# President Thomas Jefferson

Jefferson rode on horseback to his inauguration in Washington, D.C.

In 1800, Jefferson ran for president again and won. He was the third president of the United States. But he was the first to be sworn into office in Washington, D.C.

The capital was brand new then. The White House wasn't even finished yet. But Jefferson got right to work.

He bought a huge
piece of land
from France.
It was called the
Louisiana Purchase,
and it made the
U.S. twice as big.

In 1803 President
Jefferson (left) bought
the Louisiana Territory
(below) from France.
All or parts of
15 states were formed
from this land.

Sacagawea was a Shoshone. She helped
Lewis and Clark to find their way in the West.

Then he sent two men,
Lewis and Clark, out to
explore the new land.
They came back with
many maps and treasures.
They even brought
two grizzly bears.

31

Some people wanted to treat
the president like a king.
Jefferson said no.
He wore plain clothes.
He wouldn't let anyone
bow to him.

People liked Thomas Jefferson,
and in 1804 he won
a second term as president.
But by 1809, he was ready
to go back to Monticello.

Thomas
Jefferson
watching
a slave
working at
Monticello

Jefferson invented this rotating table for his files. Can you see the letters of the alphabet on each drawer?

He didn't rest much, though.
There were still many things
that he wanted to do.

# Chapter 5

# Always Doing

"It is wonderful
how much may be done,
if we are always doing."

Jefferson wrote those words
to his daughter Martha.
They were true for him.

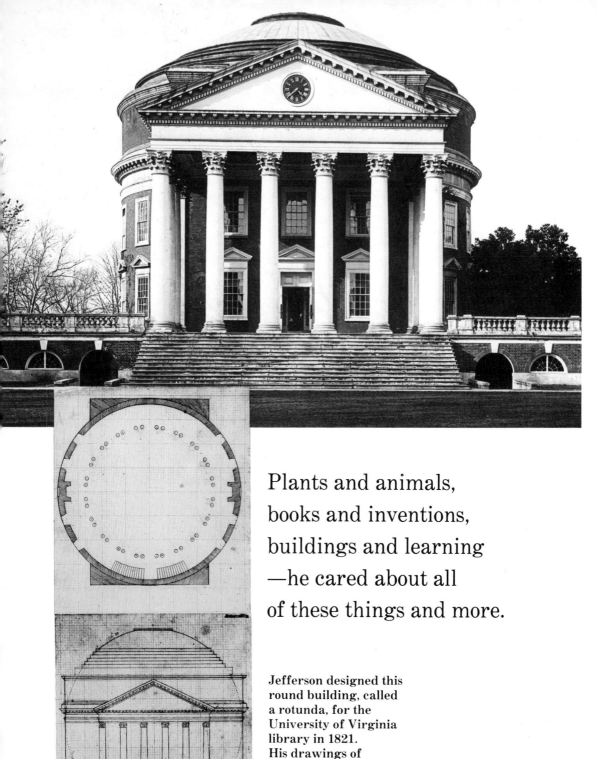

Plants and animals,
books and inventions,
buildings and learning
—he cared about all
of these things and more.

Jefferson designed this
round building, called
a rotunda, for the
University of Virginia
library in 1821.
His drawings of
the plans are seen
at the left.

He tried new ways
of planting crops
and of raising animals.

His books
became the
start of today's
Library of
Congress.

Jefferson owned
and read
books written
in French,
German, and
Latin.

Jefferson invented a machine (above) that could write two copies of a letter at the same time. He built a tiny elevator, called a "dumbwaiter" (right), to carry bottles of wine up to his dining room from the basement.

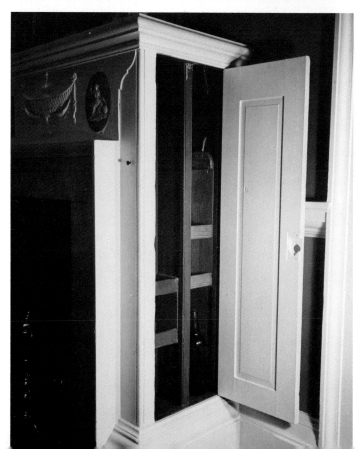

Jefferson made this comfortable chair
with a writing table attached.

He invented storm windows,
a chair that turned,
a special part for a plow,
and many other things.

The gardens (left) as well as the buildings (right, top and bottom)
at the University of Virginia were planned by Jefferson.

He wanted more people to
have a chance to learn.
So he started the
University of Virginia.
He planned the buildings
and chose the teachers.

This statue of Thomas Jefferson stands
on the grounds of the University of Virginia

Many people visited or
wrote to Jefferson.
They wanted to learn from him.
Sometimes he had to leave
his house to get some rest!

could the dead feel any interest in Monu
-ments or other remembrances of them, when, as
Anacreon says: Ολιγη δε κεισομεσθα
                    Κονις, οσεων λυθεντων
the following would be to my Manes the most
gratifying.
On the grave    a plain die or cube of 3.f without any
mouldings, surmounted by an Obelisk
of 6.f. height, each of a single stone:
on the faces of the Obelisk the following
inscription, & not a word more

Here was buried
        Thomas Jefferson
Author of the Declaration of American Independance
        of the Statute of Virginia for religious freedom
& Father of the University of Virginia.

because by these, as testimonials that I have lived, I wish most to
be remembered. ~~these~~ to be of the coarse stone of which
my columns are made, that no one might be tempted
hereafter to destroy it for the value of the materials.
my bust by Ciracchi, with the pedestal and truncated
column on which it stands, might be given to the University
if they would place it in the Dome room of the Rotunda.
on the Die, of the Obelisk might be engraved
        Born Apr. 2. 1743. O.S.
        Died ——              ,

Jefferson left this plan for his tombstone.

A life mask
of Jefferson,
made in 1825,
one year before
his death

On July 4, 1826,
Thomas Jefferson died.
It was exactly 50 years
since the Declaration
of Independence had
been adopted.

He had done so much for
his country and its people.
But he wanted them to
remember just three things.

# In CONGRESS, July 4, 1776

## The unanimous Declaration of the thirteen united States of America.

The Declaration of Independence with signatures.
Can you find Thomas Jefferson's signature?
Look under John Hancock's signature.

Jefferson wrote
the words that
are carved on
his tombstone.

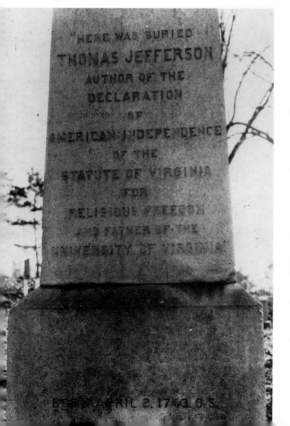

He had written the
Declaration of Independence.
He gave people in Virginia
the right to choose a religion.
He was the father of the
University of Virginia.

Today, we do remember
Thomas Jefferson for
those three things
—and many, many more.

# Important Dates

1743    April 13—Born in Albemarle County, Virginia, to Jane and Peter Jefferson

1760    Went to the College of William and Mary, Williamsburg, Virginia

1767    Became a lawyer

1769    Served in House of Burgesses, Williamsburg, Virginia

1772    Married Martha Wayles Skelton

1776    Wrote Declaration of Independence

Elected to Virginia House of Delegates

1779    Became governor of Virginia

1783    Elected to Continental Congress

1785    Became minister (later ambassador) to France

1790    Became U.S. secretary of state

1797    Became vice president of the United States

1801    Became third president of the United States

1804    Elected to a second term

1825    University of Virginia opened

1826    July 4—Died at Monticello, Virginia

## INDEX

**Page numbers in boldface type indicate illustrations.**

PHOTO CREDITS

ABOUT THE AUTHOR

Carol Greene has degrees in English literature and musicology. She has worked in international exchange programs, as an editor, and as a teacher of writing. She now lives in Webster Groves, Missouri, and writes full-time. She has published more than 100 books, including those in the Rookie Biographies series.